PRAISE FOR THE ONLINE COURSE

"Wow, I was blown away by this course. I have taken meditation training classes in the past but nothing for me compares to this course in quality and the variety of practices discussed. The graphics and music are so amazing and beautiful not to mention the wonderful soothing and comforting voice of the instructor. Take this class and learn more ways to apply your meditation practice than you ever imagined as you have fun and experience joy doing so."

— David Karg, Tutor, NFSH—The Healing Trust Training USA

"The material is well presented and the content very valuable and helpful for beginning a meditation practice."

— Jan W., artist

"I love this course: it's clear and videos are not too long. Not boring at all. It is what I was looking for."

— Paola Elena, Italy

MEDITATIONS ON THE NATURAL WORLD

ALSO BY MOLLY LARKIN

The Wind Is My Mother:
The Life and Teachings of a Native American Shaman

The Fountain of Youth Is Just a Breath Away:
Breathing Exercises for Relaxation, Health and Vitality

Ancient Journeys CD:
Three Self-Healing Meditations

Meditations

ON THE

Natural World

Find the Technique That's Right for You

A GUIDED JOURNAL

By
Molly Larkin

Published by Summit Press
P.O. Box 235
Granville, OH 43023

ISBN-13: 978-0-9983533-4-5
ISBN-10: 0998353345

Contact: Molly Larkin peace@mollylarkin.com

This book is designed as a companion piece to the online meditation course, *Meditations on the Natural World: Find the Technique That's Right for You,* which can be found at: https://mollylarkinonline.teachable.com/p/meditationsonthenaturalworld

However, this book will work perfectly on its own as a meditation primer.

Buddha was asked,
"What have you gained from meditation?"
He replied: "Nothing!
However, let me tell you what I have lost:
Anger,
Anxiety,
Depression,
Insecurity,
Fear of old age and death."

table of contents

Introduction

A few years ago, as I was walking around the lake near my home, I came upon a family of swans by the shore: two beautiful, huge adults and 10 little baby swans. Ten!

The two parents were putting up a very loud squawk. As I got closer, I saw that one of the babies had become stranded on the shore side of a big log, and the parents were encouraging it to climb over.

The baby kept trying but the log was too big and the baby too small to get over it. So the parents took turns stepping up on the log, turning around and squatting in the hopes the baby would grab on to them and be pulled out. After about a dozen attempts, they succeeded.

The irony was that if any of them had looked to the baby's left, they would have seen the much easier path to freedom was an easy swim *around* the log! But they were all too focused on the problem right in front of them to look for other solutions.

It struck me that this was a perfect example of the benefits of meditation. Stop, take a break, relax, regroup, and make space for a fresh perspective. Inspiration and new ideas usually follow.

Also, focusing on a problem is seldom the way to a solution. Or, as Albert Einstein said, "No problem can be solved from the same level of consciousness that created it."

HOW I LEARNED TO HATE MEDITATION

My own relationship with meditation had a rocky start. In my twenties, I joined a cult, which seemed like a very good idea at the time, but was hard on many levels.

One of the many disciplines we were encouraged to undertake was to meditate for one hour every morning and one hour every night.

It was virtually impossible for me. I like to be physically active and found sitting in one place for more than 5 minutes at a time very difficult. It was like asking a non-swimmer to start swimming in the deep end of the pool.

So meditation wasn't working for me in the least!

And, being a perfectionist, I felt that if I couldn't meditate for the full hour, there was no point in meditating at all, so I rarely did it!

HOW I LEARNED TO LOVE MEDITATION

Eventually, I made my way back to meditation, by finding a meditation technique that was right for me.

That's the thing: there is not one right way to meditate. There are *many* ways to meditate. The secret is to find one that works for YOU! That's why I created this book, and the accompanying course.

While I may have included a quote from the Buddha in the forward of this book, I want to assure you that you don't have to be a Buddhist, or even a spiritual person, to meditate. You can be an atheist and meditate—the goal is peace of mind and stress reduction. And we can all use that!

Meditation has been part of my morning spiritual practice for many years and my favorite part of the day. By silencing the chatter in my mind, there is space for inspiration. Just as the swans might have found the easy way out if they'd stopped their frantic rescue efforts and taken a look around, some of my best creative ideas and solutions slip in during my meditation time.

I have meditated every day since 1999, and have taught meditation in the United States, Europe and Australia. I've also studied extensively with Native American and Maya elders, and have incorporated Native meditation techniques in this book, and the accompanying online course. I'm delighted to share with you what I've learned.

I'm confident that in this book you will find the right technique for you, to reduce your stress, bring you peace of mind, increase your creativity and improve your health.

So let's get started.

CHAPTER 1

Meditation: What Is It and Why Do It?

"I have lived with several Zen masters—all of them cats."

— ECKHART TOLLE

Before reading this chapter, please answer the following questions in the space below:

What do you think meditation is?

_____

_____

_____

_____

_____

_____

_____

Have you tried it: ☐ yes   ☐ no

If not, why not?

_____

_____

_____

_____

_____

_____

_____

_____

_____

If you tried it, what was your experience? Hard? Easy? Boring?

_____

_____

_____

_____

_____

_____

_____

_____

_____

_____

JUST WHAT IS MEDITATION?

Here's one definition I like:

> "Meditation is a way for nourishing and blossoming the divine within you."
>
> **— Amit Ray**

We'll come back to this, but first I want to start by citing two studies that will help explain what meditation can do for us.

Several years ago, a study was done that estimated our brains think up to **50,000 thoughts each day, and 90% are the same as yesterday.**

There's some dispute as to the accuracy of this statistic, but even if the number is half of that, it's a heck of a lot of thoughts!

Another study published in a 2010 issue of *Science Magazine* reported that the average American adult spends 47% of their waking life "mind wandering," or not attending to the task at hand. Moreover, these periods of mind wandering were accompanied by reports of unhappiness.

WHAT DOES MEDITATION DO?

Very simply,

- Meditation helps shut out, or at least slow down, those 50,000 random thoughts and quiets both the mind and the body.
- Meditation helps us to pay attention and focus.
- Meditation helps to stop our mind wandering.
- Meditation is good for our health.

Learning to control our random thoughts helps us achieve a state of deep peace when the mind is calm and silent.

In today's world, we have a lot working against us. A big one is the feeling of time speeding up and slipping away.

But really, there are still 60 minutes in an hour and 24 hours in a day—it's more about the increasing amount of activity and rate of change that we must cope with in a day.

Currently, there are more world changing events happening in any given period of time than have ever happened before.

Eric Schmidt, former CEO of Google, said "We human beings currently create as much information in two days as we did from the dawn of civilization up through 2003!"

That was in 2003. How much more information must be inundating us today? No wonder we're overwhelmed!

Our minds can't keep up so we tend to shut down and go numb.

Our minds were not built for speed; we evolved when things were much slower. Four hundred years ago, people had a lot of time to ponder things before they had to change.

Our bodies were, and still are, designed to be in tune with the sun, the moon, the stars, the seasons, and the cycles of nature. That simplicity is what our souls long for. Meditation helps us slow down, and return to the sacred and our relationship with the natural world.

"Meditation is not a way of making your mind quiet. It's a way of entering into the quiet that's already there—buried under the 50,000 thoughts the average person thinks every day."

— Deepak Chopra

Exercises

1. Notice how much time you spend "mind wandering" during a day. Perhaps keep a timesheet or log of how you spend your day. Could some of that time be spent more productively?

2. What areas of your life could use more focus?

3. What causes you stress?

4. Would you like a way to reduce that stress?

5. Do you have health issues that are made worse by stress?

CHAPTER 2

Meditation Myths

"It's only hard if you think it is."

— MOLLY LARKIN

As a meditation teacher, I've heard a variety of reasons why people don't try meditation, or try and give up.

I would put most of the reasons under the category of myths.

MEDITATION MYTHS

- "It's hard!"

- "I can't stop my mind entirely!"

- "It takes too long!"

- "I have to sit on the floor in the lotus position!"

- "I have no time!"
- "I'm not calm enough to meditate!"
- "I'm not spiritual enough to meditate!"
- "It will take years to reap benefits!"
- "It's a religious practice!"

None of the above is true, but let's address them one at a time:

"IT'S HARD!"

If you believe it's hard, it could be. One of my favorite quotes applies here:

> "If you think you can, you can; if you think you can't, you can't. Either way you're right."
>
> **— Henry Ford**

There's a famous series of poems and pictures created in China in the 12th Century known as the Ten Ox Herding Pictures. When I was first introduced to them, they annoyed me because the poems and pictures suggest that meditation is hard.

But it just doesn't have to be. If you're trying at all, you can't do it wrong, and you will get some benefit.

"YOU HAVE TO STOP YOUR MIND!"

If you had that much mind control, you wouldn't need to meditate.

In a 10–15 minute meditation, I may have only a few seconds of a truly still mind, and I consider that a success. As my meditation teacher once said to me: it's normal to have thoughts pass through your mind, such as wanting a grilled cheese sandwich. But if you start to visualize getting up, going to the kitchen, taking out the cheese, getting the bread and grill, and starting to make the sandwich, your thoughts have taken you too far!

Approach it like listening to the radio in the car; when a song comes on you don't like, change the channel. When a thought comes in that you don't want, change the thought to whatever your meditation is focused on.

To paraphrase a famous quote:

"Thoughts will always come when you meditate, but you can stop them from nesting in your hair."

"IT TAKES TOO LONG!"

You can start with 2 minutes a day, while you're cooking your morning egg. This book will teach you how.

"I HAVE TO SIT IN THE LOTUS POSITION!"

Not true. Any comfortable position is fine, even in a chair. I don't recommend laying down because you may fall asleep, and being conscious is part of the point.

"I HAVE NO TIME!"

This book will teach you how to find the time.

"I'M NOT CALM ENOUGH!"

That's the point. Meditation will help calm you.

"I'M NOT SPIRITUAL ENOUGH!"

Meditation is not a spiritual or religious activity, (unless you want it to be). You can view it as a stress-reduction technique.

"IT WILL TAKE YEARS TO REAP BENEFITS!"

Research shows you can begin to notice results within 4–6 weeks of a regular meditation practice.

"IT'S A RELIGIOUS PRACTICE!"

It need not be religious—again, it's a stress-reduction technique that you can practice and benefit from whether you're Christian, Jewish, Muslim, Buddhist, or Atheist.

Or, you can make it the core of your spiritual practice depending on the technique you use.

Your choice.

Some of these misconceptions come from the fact that meditation is often associated with Buddhism.

Buddhist monk and peace advocate Thich Nhat Hanh addresses this quite nicely, and I think you could substitute the word "meditation" for "Buddhism."

"There is a misconception that Buddhism is a religion and that you worship Buddha. Buddhism is a practice, like yoga. You can be a Christian and practice Buddhism. I met a Catholic priest who lives in a Buddhist Monastery in France. He told me that Buddhism makes him a better Christian. I love that."

Exercises

1. How many of these myths have you believed were true?

2. Why? Where did these beliefs come from?

3. Now that you know they're myths, does it make you feel more willing to try meditation?

4. Have you had any other beliefs about meditation not on this list? What were they?

CHAPTER 3

Why Meditate? The Physical Benefits

"Meditation is a way to purify and quiet the mind, thus rejuvenating the body."

— DEEPAK CHOPRA

Learning to calm our minds can lead to success in all aspects of life: physical, mental, emotional, and social. In fact, there are so many benefits to meditation, I had to divide it into two chapters: physical and social.

The latest research suggests that up to 90% of visits to the doctor's office are stress-related, so finding a way to reduce our stress will save our health, our time and our money.

According to Harvard researcher Herbert Benson, M.D., the body's natural self-repair mechanisms are de-activated every time your body is under stress. Part of the reason is that stress produces cortisol, which inhibits certain immune cell functions.

So, anything that can reduce your stress can enhance your health, and meditation does just that.

You may have heard all this before, but a little more inspiration can't hurt.

MEDITATION HAS BEEN PROVEN TO:

- Reduce mental tension and improve outlook.
- Help lower blood pressure.
- Strengthen the heart.
- Decrease heart and respiratory rates.
- Increase blood flow.
- Help you sleep better.
- Reduce the intensity and length of allergy and asthma attacks.
- Manage chronic pain.
- Boost brain power.
- Slow down age-related brain atrophy.
- Increase NK[*] cells.

PAIN REDUCTION

New research from England helps confirm that meditation can also reduce our perception of pain. Since a great part of pain is our anticipation or perception of it, this is a huge benefit.

---

[*] Natural killer immune cells (NK cells) are a type of white blood cell that sends self-destruct messages to tumors and virus-infected cells, including cancer cells. It's known that stress, aging and pesticides can reduce our NK count.

Wake Forest Baptist Medical Center researchers found that a little over 30 minutes of meditation training can dramatically reduce the experience of pain. While morphine and pain-killers can typically reduce pain ratings by 25%, the Wake Forest study found a **40% reduction in pain** with meditation!

MEDITATION BOOSTS OUR BRAIN POWER

In recent studies, researchers at the University of California, Los Angeles found that people who meditate regularly have less age-related atrophy in all areas of the brain.

Eileen Luders, one of the UCLA researchers, states that regular meditation, over a period of years, "may slow down aging-related brain atrophy, perhaps by positively affecting the immune system. Meditation appears to be a powerful mental exercise with the potential to change the physical structure of the brain."

I think most of us would really enjoy that!

Exercises

1. Do a health survey. What health issues do you have that may be attributable to stress?

2. What health issues do you have that might be helped by regular meditation?

CHAPTER 4

Why Meditate? The Social Benefits

"It feels good. Kinda like when you have to shut your computer down, just sometimes when it goes crazy, you just shut it down and when you turn it on, it's okay again. That's what meditation is to me."

— ELLEN DEGENERES

"WE ARE ALL RELATED!"

Indigenous peoples around the world hold the belief that humans, animals and the natural world are all related. The Lakota prayer "Mitakuye Oyasin," the Hindu greeting, "Namaste" and the Maya phrase, "In Lak'esh, Ala K'in" are examples.

"Mitakuye Oyasin" is an acknowledgement that "everything in creation is my relative."

The Maya greet one another with the phrase "In Lak'esh, Ala K'in" meaning, "I am you, and you are me."

"Namaste" means: "The Divine light in me acknowledges the Divine light in you. And when you are in that place, and I am in that place, **we are as one.**"

There was even a Native American version of "Namaste" stated by the great Lakota Warrior Crazy Horse, when he said, "I salute the light within your eyes where the whole universe dwells. For when you are at that center within you and I am in that place within me, we shall be as one."

Scientists are finding there's something to that.

According to Lynne McTaggart's book, *The Field: The Quest for the Secret Force of the Universe*, quantum physicists have discovered that **everything in the universe, including the human mind and body, is connected by a vast quantum energy field**. In other words, everyone and everything is connected.

In a nutshell, quantum physicists have proved what indigenous peoples have always known.

In *Why God Won't Go Away: Brain Science and the Biology of Belief*, physicians Andrew Newberg and Eugene D'Aquili reported their research on the brains of Buddhist monks and Franciscan nuns during deep meditation or prayer.

They discovered that the portion of the brain that orients us in the physical world, helping us separate "them" from "us", essentially shuts down during deep meditation, creating a feeling of oneness and connectedness with the world around us.

So, I feel confident in saying that the more people meditate, the closer we'll get to world peace.

INCREASING LEARNING ABILITY

We're more effective learners when we relax. I know it seems counterintuitive, but taking more breaks can make us more productive. Productivity experts suggest getting up from your desk every 50 minutes to walk around the room and, yes, to meditate.

A relaxed mind is a creative mind. I get some of my best ideas during meditation. I'm not looking for them; they just come to me because there's room for them.

A high-priced attorney I used to work with was told by his biggest client that he'd pay the attorney his hourly rate to take walks on the beach and think about the case. That was a smart client. (And we won that case).

INCREASING INTUITION

Meditation is an excellent way to increase your intuition. When we live more intuitively, the world around us opens us up to things we may not have noticed before.

Intuition puts us in touch with universal flow. Logic is still available to us, but there is room for other information to step in.

In my workshops, I often send students on a "nature walk," which is a form of meditation. I suggest they put out a question to the universe, something that they've been having a hard time finding an answer to. Then they go for a walk in nature, observing the earth, the shrubs, flowers, trees, birds, insects and animals. At some point during that walk, which is a form of mindfulness, they will see something that brings an answer to their question.

I've never known it to fail!

I'm certain that if you establish a daily meditation practice, you will also find benefits in every aspect of your life.

Exercise

Think of times when you were at your most creative, or came up with solutions to problems easily. List your creative solutions. How did they come about? What were the circumstances surrounding you that led to the solution?

CHAPTER 5

Famous Meditation Experiments

"Meditation helps us slow down, and return to the sacred and our relationship with the natural world."

— MOLLY LARKIN

In 1993, the American capital, Washington, D.C., was also the murder capital of the United States.

In June–July of that year, there was an experiment to reduce violent crime in Washington, D.C. On the basis of previous research, it was hypothesized that the level of violent crime in the District of Columbia would drop significantly by having a large group of participants in Transcendental Meditation programs meditate to increase coherence and reduce stress in the District.

That summer, up to 4,000 meditators came to town, stayed in hotel rooms, and meditated.

Before the project, the Chief of Police exclaimed that the only thing that would create a 20% drop in crime would be 20 inches of snow. But the TM crime prevention project took place during blistering summer weather.

Although violent crime had been increasing for the previous 5 months, and usually peaked in the hot summer months, it decreased by 23.6% during the period the meditators were in town. After the study ended, crime began to increase again. The drop in crime could not be attributed to any other causes.

Over 22 separate studies around the world have demonstrated similar results!

So, meditation doesn't only benefit the person meditating. The peaceful energy has far reaching effects.

MEDITATION IN SCHOOLS

One Baltimore elementary school has replaced detention with meditation. Unruly students at Robert W. Coleman Elementary School in West Baltimore are sent to the Mindful Moment Room, which is filled with comfortable cushions and beanbags, and lit by glowing pink Himalayan salt lamps.

In the Mindful Moment Room, children are encouraged to practice deep breathing or mindful meditation.

The day at Coleman starts with breathing exercises over the P.A. system and ends with an after-school program where the students can learn yoga.

Students are also encouraged to talk through the misbehavior that landed them in the meditation room.

It's reported that the practice of mindful meditation has worked wonders, including improving academic performance. Traditional punishments can be isolating and frustrating, while the Mindful Moment Room allows students to relax and learn.

The school has seen zero suspensions since starting the mindful meditation program.

A 2004 study found that children diagnosed with ADHD who learned meditation with their parents twice a week, and practiced at home, had better concentration at school.

Another study found that mindfulness reduced students' anxiety during testing and boosted working memory.

It often works best to start children with movement, then breath work, followed by meditation.

Research has established the following benefits to yoga and meditation for children:

- Positive effect on academic performance.

- Eases anxiety and tension.

- Reduces anger, depression and fatigue.

- Improves stress management.

- Reduces problematic stress response.

- Enhances focus, attention, comprehension and memory.

- Reduces problematic behavior.

- Creates a calm, positive school environment.

"If every 8-year old in the world is taught meditation, we will eliminate violence from the world within one generation."

— Dalai Lama

Wouldn't that be extraordinary!

Our next chapter explains the difference between meditation and mindfulness.

CHAPTER 6

Meditation versus Mindfulness

"We meditate to silence the chatter in our minds so as to make space for inspiration."

— MOLLY LARKIN

People tend to use the terms meditation and mindfulness interchangeably, but there is a difference.

Meditation is when you intentionally set aside time to "meditate," sitting in one place and practicing your chosen technique.

Mindfulness is giving your undivided attention to what you're doing, as opposed to daydreaming or multi-tasking while doing it.

So, mindfulness can entail eating an apple and just eating the apple and nothing else. It entails consciously selecting the apple, washing it, looking closely at it, biting into it and noticing the texture, the flavor, the sound it makes as you chew it, and enjoying it with no distractions. That's mindfulness.

In today's hurry-up world, we are often multi-tasking and eating on the run. How often do we eat slowly, consciously, and silently, really paying attention to the food? That would be practicing mindfulness.

Both meditation and mindfulness entail focus—an attempt to stop, or at least slow down, the 50,000 random thoughts that may wander through our minds.

ALARMING STATISTICS

In an electronic world, we need the break. Some statistics reveal that the average American spends at least 10 hours a day looking at some sort of electronic screen. Trying to relax by watching TV actually doesn't relax us.

Mindfulness is being present, paying attention to your actions, your body and your surroundings and bringing your mind back when it wanders.

Try making one meal a week a mindfulness exercise:

- Rather than multitask while eating, just eat. Don't read, talk, watch TV or listen to music.

- Pay attention to the food, chew slowly, notice texture, smell, sight and taste.

- Eat slowly.

- Put down the fork between bites and breathe.

You'll notice your fullness levels more and will be less likely to overeat.

You can practice mindfulness while eating, exercising, gardening, washing dishes or showering.

In the shower, notice how the water flows out of the showerhead and cascades down over your body. Consciously wash and rinse your body without daydreaming. That's practicing mindfulness, being totally in the present.

In 1974, when my friend Tim Gallwey published his book, *The Inner Game of Tennis: The Classic Guide to the Mental Side of Peak Performance*, it was a phenomenon, and is still a best-selling classic today. What it really taught was mindfulness and focus.

His simple formula was to quiet the mind: observe the ball as it bounces on the way to you and hit it back, all while repeating the mantra "bounce-hit" to help keep you focused.

Being totally in the moment and focused is what makes professional athletes so good. They're in the zone, and they're likely practicing mindfulness whether they know it or not.

We delve more into mindfulness in a later chapter.

"Mindfulness isn't difficult, we just need to remember to do it."

— Sharon Salzberg

Exercise

1. Do one thing at a time for a few days, following the suggestions above.

2. Prepare one meal in the next week mindfully.

3. Eat one meal in the next week mindfully.

4. Reflect on how these mindfulness practices heighten your experience of not only the activity itself but of your day more generally. How do they change the way you feel?

CHAPTER 7
Finding Time for Meditation

"We don't need more time. We need to make better use of the time we have."

— MOLLY LARKIN

The biggest reason people give me for not meditating is: "I'm too busy. I don't have the time."

But here's another viewpoint:

"Half an hour's meditation is essential except when you are very busy. Then a full hour is needed."

— Francis de Sales

Why would he say that? It seems counter-intuitive, doesn't it?

Well actually, the less stressed you are, the more efficient you are.

Making the time to relax and meditate will help you focus and use your time better, at least that's my experience.

We don't really need more time, we need to make better use of the time we have.

And the trick is not to get more done. The trick is to decide what you really need/want to be doing and eliminate the rest. We are an over-busy society, and much of what we do doesn't add value to our lives.

Successful people know how to focus their time and energy. Being productive relies on the ability to distinguish between tasks that move you closer to your goals and tasks that don't.

Every time you're about to take on another task, ask yourself: is this the best use of my time? How will this move me toward my goals?

Here are some suggestions as to how to create more time:

Go to bed 10 minutes earlier and wake up 10 minutes earlier. Put the alarm across the room so you have to get up. Set an alarm clock and your phone alarm five minutes apart so if you sleep through one you hopefully won't sleep through the other.

Don't watch the news in the morning. It's depressing and takes time away from your morning preparation for the rest of the day. Read something inspiring instead.

Make lists. Set daily goals and prioritize them with lists of what you need to do and cross each item off as you accomplish it. Trying to keep track in your head of everything you have to do just clutters your mind.

Lists help you focus on important objectives:

- You're less likely to forget to do something important.

- Your mind will be clearer.

- You're less likely to be distracted.

- You'll feel the reward of checking off what you complete.

- You'll feel more in control.

- You'll waste less time.

Be sure to put "meditate" on your list.

Delegate. You don't really have to do it all, do you?

Spend less time on social media. I'm not saying eliminate it. Just spend less time. Set a timer for 15 minutes, after which you will have to stop.

Learn how to say, "no." You don't have to do everything asked of you.

Rest. When I was working on writing *The Wind is My Mother*, I made it a rule to take one day a week off for play and rest. It made me much more productive the other six days.

Take breaks. Get up from the computer (or whatever your task) every hour and move around. Get a drink of water.

Use a time log for a week. It will show you how you're spending your time and give insight as to how to spend it more effectively. Adjust how you spend your time after reviewing it.

Unless you're actually practicing mindfulness, why not multi-task? If you're in the waiting room at the doctor's office, come prepared with something to do, read, or write. Water the plants or dust while you talk on the phone; these are easy things to do that should still let you focus on your conversation.

When cooking, make a double batch and freeze the rest for another time.

Only check email three times a day. Be in charge of your time. Rather than letting the phone and email interrupt you at will, turn them off and check them on a break.

Remember: You're the boss of you!

If you incorporate at least some of these practices into your day, I guarantee you will have the time to meditate.

Here is one more tip you'll enjoy.

THE $25,000 PRODUCTIVITY TIP

This is one of the best productivity tips I've ever come across—and it's a true story on how to be more productive.

One-hundred years ago, Charles M. Schwab was the president of the second largest steel company in the U.S. He was visited by management consultant Ivy Ledbetter Lee, who offered to make Schwab's management team 20% more productive.

Schwab asked Lee how much he would charge and Lee replied,

"Follow my advice for 90 days, then pay me what you think my advice was worth."

At the end of 90 days, Schwab paid Lee $25,000, saying it was the most profitable advice he'd ever received. In today's dollars that might be around $500,000!

HERE'S THE ADVICE:

1. Each night make a list of the top six things you want to accomplish the next day.

2. Number them from 1–6 in order of importance.

3. The next morning, start working on task number one until you complete it. Do not move onto the next task until you complete the one before.

4. Any tasks left at the end of the day get moved to the top of the next day's list.

The list always stays with six items on it. The key is to prioritize and focus.

So that's it. Try it for 90 days and see how your life changes.

"A most useful approach to meditation practice is to consider it the most important activity of each day. Schedule it as you would an extremely important appointment, and unfailingly keep your appointment."

— **Roy Eugene Davis**

Exercise

Pick one of the suggestions in this chapter and try it for one week. What was the result?

CHAPTER 8

The Power of Place: Home Altars

"Create a calm space and it will, in turn, calm you."

— **MOLLY LARKIN**

If you would like to jump-start your meditation practice or have an instant dose of serenity, a home altar might be just the thing to help you.

Many people think of altars as something only found in a church or sanctuary, but they don't have to be limited to that.

The right place can make all the difference to what you want to do. How well could you work without an office? Could you cook without a kitchen?

By the same token, we can benefit greatly from a designated place for our meditation practice:

- A place that is not cluttered.

- A place that evokes serenity and helps us feel calm as
  soon as we approach it.

WHAT IS AN ALTAR?

Altars are created to hold focused energy, and help us to feel centered when we approach them. They represent our intention to create more serenity, peace and love in our space and our lives.

Again, this doesn't have to be spiritual or religious. It's just having a designated place to meditate.

An altar can also be a place to reflect on your personal and spiritual goals, or to honor someone or something.

Just as major religious services have altars, every indigenous ceremony has an altar to honor the spiritual realm and the gifts of the Creator. The altar is the heart of the ceremony. It also serves as a portal, a doorway, to invite the good spirits in.

You can have more than one altar, in any room of the house, or even outdoors. I have an altar at my outdoor well to give thanks for the water that comes to my home from the earth.

Any place where you want to be reminded to stop, reflect, breathe and be grateful is appropriate.

I think the bathroom is an excellent place for an altar for water. Think about it: water is the first thing we use in the morning and the last thing we use at night. Being able to turn a handle and have water (either hot or cold) pour forth is like a miracle to many people in the world. Be grateful for it!

The bathroom is also the place where we cleanse ourselves, maintain our health, and rid ourselves of toxins and negative energies. It's one of the most important rooms in the house, so it might be good to honor it as such.

> "Think of an altar as a physical manifestation of your inner spiritual landscape. Artfully laden with images and objects that remind you of your own best self, an altar gives you the opportunity to consciously reflect on things you might otherwise take for granted. It's a place of solace and repose that becomes a receptacle for your spiritual energy. And when you sit before it, that energy is reflected back to you."
>
> **— Lauren Ladoceour**

STEPS FOR CREATING AN ALTAR

1. If you will be meditating and/or praying at your altar, select a location that will give you the privacy you need.

2. Identify the space and clear it of clutter and old energy: smudge [purify] with incense or sage. Vacuum and dust well.

3. Keep it simple and clean. This is where you will pray, meditate, and perhaps journal.

4. Select sacred items to place on it.

THINGS YOU MIGHT HAVE ON AN ALTAR

- Photos/statues of spiritual teachers or your loved ones

who watch over you, or those who have the qualities you wish to emulate.

- Inspiring books/quotes to refer to.

- Crystals or special rocks.

- Plants or flowers.

- Candles.

- Incense.

- Anything else that is meaningful to you.

HOW TO MAINTAIN AN ALTAR

- Renew your altar on every New Moon, as this is the time of new beginnings.

- Clean it regularly. Don't let it get dusty. An altar is a reflection of your life, so take good care of it.

HOW TO USE YOUR ALTAR

- Pray or meditate at your altar daily, as this will help raise the energy there. In that way, each time you approach it, you will automatically tune into that energy of serenity.

- It can be an excellent practice to start and end your day there!

"Like a fireplace, the altar is a hearth to me. It's where I go to kindle my soul and my connection to what is meaningful and inspiring."

— **Sean Johnson**

Exercise

1. Create an altar using the steps outlined above.

2. Reflect on how you feel about your altar and its place in your home.

3. If you've started using it, how does it change your experience of praying, meditating, contemplating, and/or journaling? Is there something else you do at your altar that helps you find an energy of serenity?

CHAPTER 9

Creating Good Habits

"You will never change your life until you change something you do daily."

— MIKE MURDOCK

No course on meditation could be complete without a lesson on forming good habits. Because regular meditation is, after all, a habit. And once you have applied the habit lesson to meditation, you can apply it to other aspects of your life.

Forming good habits will benefit you in myriad ways. If you want to be successful in any endeavor, you must be able to control your mind, limit the 50,000 random daily thoughts, and concentrate on how to achieve your outcome with no distractions.

"The most important moment of any habit is the starting... It's that simple. Focus on the moment of starting,
tell yourself you don't have to do anything else, and then
do that one moment with the intention of love."

— Leo Baubauta

Believe you can and you will.

Consistency is the key to forming new habits.

Start small so you can have success. Remember my failure when I
was supposed to meditate one hour every morning and one hour every
evening? It was just too much for a beginner. Start small, even just two
minutes a day.

You are building habit muscles, just as if you were starting an exercise program. Because you are! Small wins will build your confidence
and cement the habit.

Commit to at least two minutes a day for a week, then increase to
5 minutes for another week, then 10 minutes, etc.

And try to do it the same time every day.

Two minutes is an easy commitment to make, and small wins will
build your confidence and cement the habit.

FIND THE MOTIVATION

It's important that you want to do it; don't feel you have to do it.

Go back to Chapters 3 and 4 on reasons to meditate and choose
a motivating reason to do it. If you've gotten this far in the book, you
clearly want to have a regular meditation practice. Congratulations on
that decision.

If it's for health reasons, let's say lowering your blood pressure, write your ideal blood pressure on Post-its and put them where you'll see them: in the bathroom, in your meditation space, in the kitchen, or anywhere you could use the reminder.

HERE ARE MORE TIPS

Practice at the **same time every day** and ensure you will not be disturbed.

If possible, **close the door and turn off the phone.** At work, if you don't have a door to close, go to your car on a break. Set an alarm with a gentle tone for 2–5 minutes. (The exception would be if you're using one of the more active meditation techniques presented later in the book.)

Select a trigger to associate with morning meditation, such as: get up, go to the bathroom, sit and meditate. That's your new routine. That's mine and it's worked since 1999. If you tell yourself you'll do it later, later just might never come. First thing in the morning is the ideal time to do it.

Give yourself reminders. Put Post-its on the bathroom mirror, closet door or coffee maker that say, "meditate".

Do it in the same place each day. Find a quiet spot. Create a corner of your bedroom with a comfy pillow or chair, create an altar, or go into the garden or a park. Choose someplace peaceful where you won't be disturbed. You could also go for a walk and do a moving meditation (See, Chapter 22).

Be comfortable. Sitting in the lotus position is not necessary. Be comfortable above all. Sit on a pillow or chair, or even stand. All that matters is that you are comfortable. I don't recommend lying down as it's too likely you'll fall asleep.

Posture. Sit comfortably, with the spine straight and the head balanced, palms resting comfortably on your lap.

Commit to doing this for **30 days**.

Another thing that can help is to do it with a friend. **Accountability** makes a huge difference. Check in with one another each day.

Congratulate yourself each time you do it.

Have consequences. One consequence is that people may respect you less if you don't do what you said you would. You may also think less of yourself. I'll sometimes give myself consequences such as: I if I don't do _____, I can't have any chocolate today. (Chocolate is a big motivator for me.)

Or, even better, reward yourself when you've meditated every day for a week.

If you miss a day, recognize why and find the solution to avoid having the problem again.

Try not to miss two days in a row, because it will make it harder to start up again. If you're running late and can't sit, do some focused, slow breathing in the car or bus on the way to work.

"Are you experiencing restlessness? Stay!
Are fear and loathing out of control? Stay!
Aching knees and throbbing back? Stay!
What's for lunch? Stay!
I can't stand this another minute! Stay!"

— Pema Chödrön

At other times of the day, visualize yourself meditating; see yourself as a calm person because you meditate. Changing your self-image can be a huge help.

"Sow a thought, and you reap an act.
Sow an act, and you reap a habit.
Sow a habit, and you reap a character.
Sow a character, and you reap a destiny."

— Samuel Smiles

Exercise

1. Review chapters 3 and 4 and decide what your motivation is for meditation. Why do you want to do it? What will the consequences be if you don't and if you do?

2. Meditate for two minutes minimum every day this week. How does it feel?

CHAPTER 10

Tips on Starting a Meditation Practice

"Do not wait. The time will never be 'just right.'"

— MOLLY LARKIN

This chapter is somewhat duplicative because you can't get enough reminders of the why and how to meditate!

Meditation will ideally be one of the first things you do in a day, even before eating or checking email.

Do it in the same spot daily.

First thing in the morning is the ideal time to do it. It will set the tone for a great day. If you can't do it in the morning, do it whenever you can make the time.

It's ideal to practice at the same time every day and ensure you will not be disturbed. If possible, lower the lights, close the door and turn off the phone. Do your best to eliminate interruptions.

At work, if you don't have a door to close, go to your car. (Unless you're practicing one of the moving or outdoor meditations presented in the later part of this book.)

Select a trigger to associate with morning meditation, such as:

- Get up.

- Go to the bathroom.

- Sit.

- Meditate.

Deepak Chopra uses the acronym RPM: Rise-Pee-Meditate.

That's your new routine. That's mine and it's worked since 1999. If you tell yourself you'll do it later, later just might never come.

Give yourself reminders: put Post-its on the bathroom mirror, closet door, coffee maker, all around the house, if necessary, saying: "meditate."

Set an alarm with a gentle tone for 2–5 minutes.

Create a quiet spot for meditation. We discussed this in *Chapter 8, The Power of Place*: by having a designated place to meditate, it helps you get in the proper mood as soon as you sit there. It should also be a decluttered spot. Trying to meditate in between piles of books or laundry won't be relaxing.

Perhaps create a corner of your bedroom with a comfy pillow or chair, create an altar, or go into the garden or a park. Go someplace peaceful where you won't be disturbed. You could also go for a walk and do a moving meditation, as discussed in Chapter 22.

Above all, be comfortable; sitting in the lotus position is not mandatory. Sit on a pillow or chair, or even stand. All that matters is that you are comfortable and the spine is straight, hands resting comfortably on your lap. I don't recommend lying down as it's too likely you'll fall asleep.

Close your eyes or have a soft focus on something pleasant to look at, perhaps something on your altar.

At other times of the day, visualize yourself meditating; see yourself as a calm person because you meditate. Changing your self-image can be a huge help.

Start with focusing on breathing—Chapter 11 of this workbook presents breathing meditations. You might also want to get my book, *The Fountain of Youth Is Just a Breath Away: Breathing Exercises for Relaxation, Health and Vitality*, which has a variety of breathing exercises.

Sit with a smile on your face.

Have a beginner's mind: no preconceptions, no judgment, no self-judgment, be open.

Your mind is likely to get distracted. Just change the channel or the thought, the same way you would change the channel if a song you didn't like came on the radio.

Most of all, know that you haven't failed if extraneous thoughts come in; it's part of the process. One second of deep peace is more than worth the other 15 minutes or so of passing thoughts, I guarantee it. I used to hate meditation; now it's the highlight of my day. Put another way:

> "You cannot keep birds from flying over your head, but you can prevent them from nesting in your hair."
>
> **— Martin Luther**

And, last but far from least, always say "Thank you" for whatever experience you have. Appreciation always brings more positive experiences.

To find the time to meditate, refer back to Chapter 7 on creating more time in the day.

"A year from now you will wish you had started today."

— Karen Lamb

Exercise

1. How did you fare with each of the above suggestions?

2. Which were your favorite "tips?"

3. How did they help?

CHAPTER 11

Meditation on the Breath

"Trees breathe, and in the process purify the air around them. Be like a tree, still and breathing."

— MOLLY LARKIN

If you don't yet have a meditation practice, focusing on the breath is a great place to start. It's also one of the healthiest practices you can undertake.

My book, *The Fountain of Youth Is Just a Breath Away: Breathing Exercises for Relaxation, Health and Vitality,* goes into excellent detail on how to breathe. However, I'll cover the highlights for breath work as a meditation here.

A good start would be to observe your breath for 2–5 minutes once a day, sitting with a straight spine, eyes gently closed.

This can be done at any time:

- While driving in your car (with your eyes open, of course).

- In the supermarket line.

- In the doctor's waiting room, etc.

Most people in the west breathe shallowly and too fast. Taking time to breathe slowly brings a whole host of benefits.

When stressed, stop and pay attention to your breath. Focus your mind on the present moment.

Research has shown that good breathing can bring the same benefits as meditation:

- Increases energy.

- Lowers blood pressure.

- Improves circulation.

- Alleviates anxiety disorders without drugs.

- Helps digestion.

- Helps improve sleep.

- Helps the nervous system to function more smoothly.

- Reduces pain.

- Reduces stress.

- Improves skin and reduces facial wrinkles.

- Helps weight control as extra oxygen burns excess fat more easily.

PAYING ATTENTION TO THE BREATH

To the Maya, the most sacred salutation is for all parties to take three breaths together, in and out.

There are traditions in Asia that say you can reach enlightenment by doing nothing other than observing your breath.

Paying attention, or observation, is a lost art in Western society, but it's how native people for millennia knew where to find food, what weather was coming, and where danger lay.

Observation is also the key to building intuition. In modern society we are over-stimulated and, as a result, want to shut out as much as we can. The downside is that we miss a lot. We miss subtle changes in the weather, traffic patterns, our health, and the natural world.

The Nature Walk described in Chapter 4 is a prime example of observation that can help open your intuition. But, back to the breath.

A CONSCIOUS BREATHING MEDITATION

1. Place one hand on the abdomen, and the other on your chest. Take a deep, slow inhale through the nostrils, making sure the abdomen expands out more than the chest. This ensures that the base of the lungs is getting air.

2. Exhale.

3. Inhale through the nose to a count of 4, letting the abdomen rise.

4. Slowly exhale to a count of 6, while contracting your abdominal muscles to assist the expulsion of air.

5. Repeat this cycle four more times for a total of 5 deep inhales/exhales. You ideally want to work up to breathing at a rate of one breath every 10 seconds (or six breaths a minute).

Count as you do it. The act of counting will engage your mind, taking it away from random thoughts.

Practice breathing consciously throughout the day, any time you feel the desire to be calmer and slow down, making your breath deeper, slower, quieter, and more regular.

If we become upset, our breath may become shallow, rapid, noisy and irregular. Changing how we breathe can change our physiology and will help to calm us down.

We know that trees breathe, and in the process purify the air around them. Be like a tree, still and breathing.

Smokers say smoking calms them down. Well, I think it calms them because they're taking a long, deep inhale and a slow exhale (while feeding their addiction, of course). It's the slow breathing that is calming. They could get results from just doing that and forget the cigarette.

You'll find many breathing techniques in my book, *The Fountain of Youth is Just a Breath Away: Breathing Exercises for Relaxation, Health and Vitality*.

A daily breathing practice is one of the best things you can do for health, relaxation and meditation.

"If I had to limit my advice on healthier living to just one tip, it would be simply to learn how to breathe correctly."
— **Andrew Weil, M.D.**

Exercise

1. Practice the conscious breathing exercise described above for five days in a row.

2. Reflect on how it makes you feel. Do you see any changes with each day that passes? How do you feel after practicing for five days in a row?

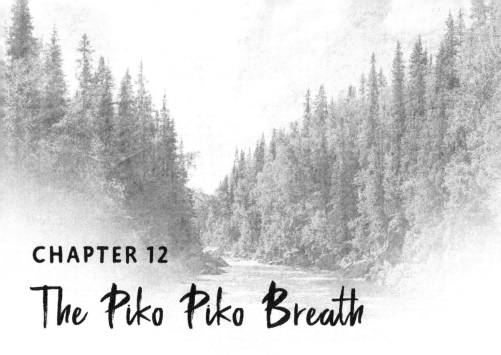

CHAPTER 12
The Piko Piko Breath

"Our bodies were designed to be in tune with the sun, the moon, the stars, and the cycles of nature. That simplicity is what our souls long for. Meditation takes you there."

— MOLLY LARKIN

There may be no easier way to rise above the daily grind than through breath work, and the Piko Piko Breath is one of the best ways I've found.

Kahunas, the shamanic practitioners of Hawaii, use the Piko Piko Breath to both relax and energize the body. It can work for anyone, and can give a real sense of the expansiveness of the universe.

The word "Piko" means center, or naval.

Before Kahunas meditate or pray, they use this breath to build up their Mana (Power) in order to get focused and in the right frame of mind for whatever they are about to undertake, particularly healing.

If you've been to Hawaii or watched the television show *Hawaii Five-0*, you know that Caucasians in Hawaii are referred to as "haoles" (pronounced "howlies") which means "without breath." This is because the Kahunas know that most Caucasians have lost the ability to do healthy, deep, slow breathing.

Why? Because modern life is full of stress, and our bodies are usually too tense to remember to breathe correctly.

Also, in the words of Andrew Weil, M.D.: "We're a country obsessed with flat stomachs. But tight, rigid abdominal muscles crimp the action of the diaphragm, which needs to move easily in order to breathe."

Piko Piko breathing is a method of releasing tension and relaxing the body by bringing your awareness to different areas of both the body and the natural world.

Focusing attention while breathing allows for deeper breathing to take place, which enhances health, and puts one in a meditative state.

Also, breathing from and to various areas creates a beautiful ball of energy around the body, and helps you feel connected to the cosmos.

THE PRACTICE

1. Sit comfortably with your spine straight, arms and legs uncrossed, and your hands resting comfortably on your lap. As you practice this breath technique over time, try to lengthen the inhale and exhale.

2. Inhale through your nose, allowing the abdomen to expand, and exhale through your mouth, allowing the abdomen to fall. Repeat.

3. Place your attention at the top of your head, and feel a connection to all that is above you. Visualize breathing

in through the top of your head. Then visualize breathing out through the navel. Repeat.

4. Visualize breathing in the stars from above. Then visualize breathing out through your feet to the earth below. Repeat.

5. Visualize breathing in through the shoulders. Visualize breathing out to the earth below. Repeat.

6. Visualize breathing in the horizon. Visualize breathing out the navel. Repeat.

7. Visualize breathing in the future from above. Visualize breathing out the past through your feet. Repeat.

8. Now start to move your fingers and toes, and rub your hands on your legs to bring back sensation.

This is a good breathing technique for helping you feel centered and connected to nature and the cosmos. Use it any time you feel you need centering, or before healing . . . or any time at all.

Exercise

1. Practice the Piko Piko breath at least once in the next week.

2. Observe and reflect on any sensations you experience with this practice. Do you find that you feel more centered and connected? Did you have any challenges? Is this a practice you would like to continue doing?

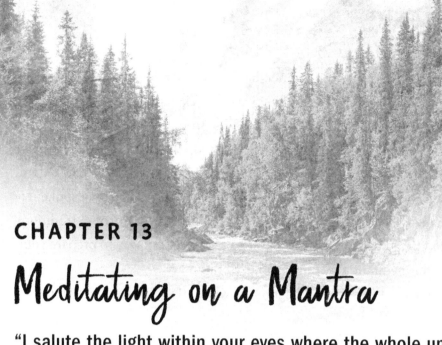

CHAPTER 13
Meditating on a Mantra

"I salute the light within your eyes where the whole universe dwells. For when you are at that center within you and I am in that place within me, we shall be as one."

— CRAZY HORSE, LAKOTA SIOUX WARRIOR

Many people associate meditation with having a mantra, which is a sacred word or phrase. While repeating a mantra is one way to meditate, it's not the only way.

Mantra meditation was the first meditation technique that really worked for me, particularly when the teacher said I could do it just 10 minutes a day.

A mantra is simply a statement or word repeated over and over. It's a way to focus your mind on something other than those 50,000 random thoughts.

There are many organizations and instructors that teach meditation and will give you a mantra. Or you can simply choose any word as your mantra and focus on it. Remember that the whole point is to focus your mind away from those random 50,000 thoughts.

I'm going to suggest you choose one from the Bija Mantras.

The word 'bija' in Sanskrit means 'seed'. The Bija Mantras originated in India and are the seed sounds of each chakra (energy center), helping us move to higher states of consciousness. When whispered, spoken, or chanted they can activate and balance life energy. In some traditions, one might chant all the Bija Mantras as a powerful way to prepare yourself for meditation by raising your vibration.

First, let's look at a diagram of where the seven main chakras are located on the human body.

I want to emphasize that we could do an entire course on just the chakras, so this is just a simple overview in order to introduce the Bija Mantras.

Here's a chart of the chakras (energy centers) and their associated qualities. If there's a particular area of your life you feel you need to develop or heal, chanting the Bija Mantra associated with the relevant chakra will give you a start.

There are actually hundreds of energy centers in the body, but we'll focus on the seven main chakras:

	Chakra	Color	Associated Emotional Functions	Mantra
7th	Crown	Violet	Spirituality, Connection with a Higher Power	OM (aum)
6th	Third Eye	Indigo	Intuition; mental functioning	Sham (Shaaamm)
5th	Throat	Blue	Communication	Ham (Haaam-mm)
4th	Heart	Green	Love and compassion	Yam (Yaaam-mm)
3rd	Solar Plexus	Yellow	Self-esteem; emotional balance; knowing our place in the universe	Ram (Raaam-mm)
2nd	Sacral	Orange	Sexual energy, creativity, joy	Vam (Vaaaaamm)
1st	Root	Red	Sexuality; connection to our ancestors, safety, grounding	Lam (Laaam-mm)

So, choose any one to start, and repeat it over and over.

You can say them all, or just focus on one. Let's say you want to focus on opening up your heart. You would repeat the mantra 'Yam' over and over to yourself during your meditation time.

You can also repeat it silently, in your head, bringing your mind back when your mind wanders away. It's merely a focusing tool. Feel free to play gentle music at the same time, to relax you. It's that simple.

Exercise

Choose a mantra and use it as your meditation focus for at least two days in the next week. Observe and reflect on how it makes you feel.

CHAPTER 14

Mindfulness in Daily Life

"Don't let a wandering mind control your life. Learn to control your mind through meditation."

— MOLLY LARKIN

Mindfulness is moment-to-moment awareness, focusing on what you're doing, and trying to keep your mind from wandering. It's purposefully paying attention to things we normally never give a moment's thought to—things we often do while multitasking.

The fact is, multitasking is not as productive as we think. Our brains aren't equipped for multitasking those tasks that require brainpower. Our short-term memories can only store between five and nine things at once. When you're trying to accomplish two dissimilar tasks, each one requiring some level of consideration and attention, multitasking is counterproductive.

When you multitask, you actually don't work faster, your stress level soars, and you're limiting your short-term memory and creativity. It's fine for simple tasks—I can dust and talk on the phone with the best of them. But multitasking isn't effective for serious work.

Now back to mindfulness:

How often do we daydream or let our minds wander while doing an everyday task such as washing the dishes? What if we didn't let our minds wander, but rather focused on the task at hand, clearing the mind of all other thoughts. That would, indeed, be profoundly restful and relaxing.

Earlier, I mentioned practicing mindfulness while eating an apple. In addition to eating, one can mindfully wash the dishes, sweep the floor, make the bed, prepare a meal, listen to music, or eat a meal, and much more.

To mindfully eat an apple, do only the following, without multi-tasking; stay aware of your breathing, your inhales and exhales throughout.

1. Select an apple.

2. Wash it.

3. Dry it.

4. Look at it and give it your undivided attention.

5. What kind of apple is it?

6. Where did it grow?

7. What color is it?

8. What is its shape and size?

9. How does it feel in your hand?

10. What does it smell like?

11. Take a bite and chew slowly.

    i.   What sound does it make as you chew?

    ii. What does it feel like in your mouth?

    iii. Chew slowly and savor the taste.

As you become fully aware of eating the apple, you become fully aware of the present moment. You become more alive.

This is practicing mindfulness.

In *The Wind Is My Mother; The Life and Teachings of a Native American Shaman*, Bear Heart teaches about the Native American practice of eating in silence, without television or conversation:

"You need to pay attention to your stomach, what you're putting into it and how you're doing it because your stomach is your biggest help. It's where the energy that sustains your life enters your body. You think you save a lot of time by working while you eat, but then you don't understand why you feel tired and have such bad indigestion. No wonder so many executives have ulcers."

Just focus on the blessing of the food and nourishment you're receiving.

Visualize it going through your body and creating health and well-being. That's mindful eating.

THE JAPANESE TEA CEREMONY

The Japanese tea ceremony, also known as "The Way of Tea", is a beautiful example of mindfulness and finding the sacred in everyday life.

Whether gazing out the window, or going through the formality of a Japanese tea ceremony, there is tranquility and grace to be found in mindfully drinking a cup of tea (or coffee, or anything).

It's also worth noting, the Japanese reputedly have the lowest rate of heart disease in the world. Diet is a big part of that, but also, 50% of Japanese drink three cups of green tea each day! There are over 1000 studies showing that green tea helps prevent heart disease.

Dating back to the 16th Century, "The Way of Tea" developed as a path to spiritual awakening characterized by humility, grace, restraint, and simplicity.

This is a far cry from the modern practice of pouring hot water over a tea bag and drinking tea on the run. I'm embarrassed to admit I do this all too often.

Traditionally, a tea host or hostess may spend decades mastering the ceremony. They learn not just how to serve tea, but also an appreciation of art, crafts, poetry and calligraphy, flower arranging and cooking. They also learn grace and attentiveness to the needs of others.

There is also focus on creating beauty in the tea environment, and how to converse on the beauty of nature. The purpose is to delight the senses.

Guests will not engage in small talk or gossip.

The purpose of a tea gathering is to live in this moment, and not be distracted by mundane thoughts.

It's a practice in mindfulness.

The students studying the Tea Ceremony learn to think of others first. Learning is experiential, not from a book. The goal is to attain presence of mind. "The Way of Tea" is not a course to be completed, but a way of life itself.

It's about the beauty of simplicity.

The traditional tea ceremony is a spiritual experience embodying harmony, respect, purity and tranquility. Guests enter by walking across roji (Japanese for dewy ground), symbolically ridding themselves of the dust of the world. Then they wash their hands and mouths from water in a stone basin as a last purifying step.

The host receives the guests through a low door or gate, forcing them to bow upon entry—a reminder to be humble. The doorway also symbolizes leaving behind the material world and entering the spiritual world.

For an informal ceremony, guests are served sweets and tea. A formal ceremony will include a full meal and can take up to four hours.

It is an art and one may study for a long time to be qualified to do it correctly.

In Japan, people may choose to take classes or join clubs dedicated to teaching this tradition. Students learn the common hosting duties such as:

- How to properly enter and exit the tea room.
- When to bow.
- How to make the tea correctly.
- Proper placement and cleaning of the utensils and equipment.
- Appropriate guest behavior like handling and drinking from the tea bowl.

It reminds me of many indigenous ceremonies, which are all designed to bring us closer to God and to appreciate the simple beauty of this magnificent creation.

Honoring guests is a time-honored tradition in many cultures—bringing beauty and kindness into every day life.

It's not necessary to conduct a formal tea ceremony in order to experience tranquility, mindfulness and share joy with friends. One can do that with any meal, or even a simple cup of tea. Why not try it?

Exercise

Prepare a cup of tea or coffee mindfully. The instructions I'll give here will be for a cup of tea, but can apply equally well to preparing a cup of coffee.

Make a ceremony of it. Turn off the TV or radio or other distractions. Do it silently, without conversation, other than to invite whoever else is with you to join you for tea.

Prepare your instruments:

1. Choose the type of tea you would like to drink, and any sweetener or milk.
2. Clean your best tea cup.
3. Place the tea (bag) in the cup.
4. Mindfully pour water into the tea kettle.
5. Patiently breathe while it boils. Listen as the sound of the water changes as it prepares to boil.
6. Mindfully pour the boiled water into the cup with the tea.
7. Mindfully breathe while it steeps.
8. Add your sweetener/milk.
9. With total focus, sit down and take your first sip of tea.

    i.   How does it taste?

    ii. How does it feel as you swallow it?

Put out a thought of gratitude for having taken a moment from your busy day to enjoy a simple cup of tea.

There, you have practiced mindfulness while preparing and drinking a cup of tea. Congratulations! If you'd like to describe the experience or make notes on the practice, do so now.

CHAPTER 15
Mindfulness Meditation on a Rock

"Become calm and steady, like a rock. There is your superpower."

— MOLLY LARKIN

Here is another meditation practice to try. Like the practice of eating an apple or making/drinking tea, this one encourages you to be mindful of an object.

1. Find a rock from outside, or use a piece of fruit. Use any rock that will fit in the palm of your hand.

2. Assume a comfortable meditation position, with a straight spine, and place the rock in your hand.

3. Do some slow, deep breathing.

4. When your breathing is comfortably regular, explore

the rock in your hand, using your fingers. Breathe and explore.

5. Let extraneous thoughts come and go, and return your attention to the rock.

6. Run your fingers over it, feel its shape … it's texture … it's temperature.

    i. Are some spots smoother than others?

    ii. Are some warmer or cooler than others?

    iii. Can you feel its color? With your eyes closed, does it feel like another color?

    iv. Focus your attention on the area of your hand touching the rock. How does it feel compared to the part of your hand not touching the rock?

7. Continue to breathe and explore.

There, now you have practiced a mindfulness meditation while holding an object, like a rock or a piece of fruit. Congratulations! If you'd like to describe the experience or make notes on this practice, do so now.

CHAPTER 16

Chanting

"Ah, music, sacred tongue of God! I hear thee calling and I come."

— **CONFUCIUS**

Of all the sound-making devices and instruments found on this planet, the human voice is believed by many to have the most healing qualities. Ultimately, it can have the same positive effects as meditation.

Chanting is so powerful in creating a healing vibration that many Native American medicine people chant over patients in order to induce healing in the body. They also will chant over herbs they're going to use in healing. Chanting over the herbs can actually change the molecular structure of the herb, so that it will work most effectively for the condition it's going to treat.

Chants are chemically metabolized into endogenous opiates that are both internal painkillers as well as healing agents in the body.

Music in general has a powerful positive influence on the protective cells of the immune system. The following remarkable story serves as an example.

In the late 1960s, French physician Alfred Tomatis was called in to a Benedictine monastery in the south of France because many of the monks were suffering from a rare and undiagnosed illness; they were inexplicably exhausted and unable to perform their daily tasks. Doctors were stumped so they called in Dr. Tomatis, recognized by the French Academy of Science and Medicine for his research in healing and sound.

Tomatis discovered that in the wake of Vatican II reforms instituted by the Catholic Church in the mid-1960s, the new abbot decreed the brothers should abandon their traditional practice of singing Gregorian chants 6–8 hours a day.

Tomatis, who's been called the "Einstein of sound," surmised that the chanting had functioned as a way to energize the monks by "wakening their field of consciousness." He suggested they start chanting again. They did so, and within five months were fully recovered.

THE SOUND OF OM

There is a reason many yoga classes begin and end with the chanting of OM. OM is the most universally used chant for opening and balancing the energy centers of the human body, also known as chakras. It connects us to the infinite vibration from which our universe emerged.

OM is known as the universal sound of perfection. Chanting OM vibrates at the frequency of 432 hz, which is the vibrational frequency of everything in nature. So, it is the sound of the universe—part of the natural world.

I want to emphasize that chanting OM is not a religious practice, unless you want it to be.

Scientists have measured the sound of the earth spinning on its axis and it's the sound of OM—both sounds resonate at the same frequency. Buddhists teach that enlightenment can be reached just through the chanting of OM. It's considered to be the sound of creation.

Research has found that saying the OM sound before surgery helps in preparation and recovery. Chanting OM creates a vibration in the body that's very healing and relaxing.

So chanting OM several times can be a very centering form of meditation, or a good thing to do to prepare you for meditation.

Chanting OM in a group is an excellent way to unite everyone. People don't have to start and stop together. Just chant in your own time and let it be a continuous sound by the group.

How to chant OM

1. Chanted correctly, it consists of three syllables: A, U, M.

2. The first syllable, A, is pronounced as a long "aw." As you start at the back of your throat, expect to feel a vibration in your chest.

3. The second syllable, U, is pronounced as a long "oo." Your throat should vibrate as you make this sound.

4. The third syllable, M, is pronounced as a long "mmmmm" with your tongue gently touching the back of your front teeth.

5. Inhale through the nose, and exhale while chanting OM. When your breath ends, pause ever so briefly and repeat.

6. Seven OMs in a row is a good place to start. When done together with a group of people, as in a yoga class, it creates a very powerful vibration. It also sets you up for an excellent meditation.

Exercise

Try chanting OM and see how it makes you feel. If you're not sure what it sounds like or how to do it, my online course has a recording of monks chanting OM that you can join. You can also search for OM chanting on YouTube to get familiar with it, either listening or chanting along.

It is NOT necessary to chant in step with any recordings, in case they hold the note longer than you are comfortable with.

In fact, a common way for group chanting of OM is for people to start and stop in their own time, so that there's a continuous group tone.

Give it a try and, afterward, record your experience of the bodily sensations resulting from the vibration of energy in this chant. Did you feel more centered for a meditation practice after the chant? Did you feel more energetic, like the Benedictine monks might feel after their chanting? Was there anything that kept you from fully experiencing the chant?

CHAPTER 17

Meditating on Music

"Music is the mediator between the life of the senses and the life of the spirit."

— BEETHOVEN

How often have we been entranced by, and relaxed to, a soothing piece of music? It makes sense that listening to music we like can be a wonderful way to meditate if it puts you in a focused state.

It can speak directly to the heart, relax us, and raise our spirits, which is the point of meditation.

But does it have to be soothing music? No.

The latest scientific research on music therapy is that listening to music is healing when you enjoy the music you're listening to. If that's rock and roll, so be it.

By all means listen to whatever relaxes you at the end of a hard day. Perhaps that will then get you ready for a regular meditation practice.

But you may choose to meditate on the music itself. And that's fine, particularly if it gets you out of your wandering, 50,000-thought mind.

I think that too often we consider music a background for other activities. How often do we just listen, as in a mindfulness exercise?

The point is to listen, to feel it in your body. Let it transport you to another realm.

Music in native cultures is more than entertainment. It has a role in ritual and in tapping into the source energy which creates wellness and vitality.

However, traditional Buddhist meditation does not include music while sitting in meditation, or focusing on the breath. Listening to relaxing music while getting a massage or healing session is more of a modern movement. It's become termed "meditation music" and that may give people the notion that it's to be played during meditation. But classic meditation is meant to be done in silence.

If you want to meditate on music alone, take it seriously and don't do anything else.

To make a meditation out of listening to music, start by being mindful and paying attention the same way you'd pay attention to a mantra or your breath. When your mind wanders, return to the music.

Turn off your phone, lower the lights, get comfortable and just listen.

You can also meditate listening to natural sounds, such as water, wind, or singing birds. For people who live in cities where the sounds of nature are rare, a recording of nature sounds could be a lovely meditation. I live in the country and in the spring, after a long, hard winter, I love to open the windows and meditate on the birdsong.

If it can transport us out of a cluttered mind, it has done its job.

Exercise

1. Choose a piece of music to listen to as a meditation. Sit with a straight spine, hands resting comfortably on your lap and just listen without doing anything else.

2. Observe and reflect on what was it like to meditate on music. How did it compare to other forms of meditation you have tried so far? Is it a practice you would like to continue?

CHAPTER 18
Guided Visualization

"See it and you can be it."

— MOLLY LARKIN

Guided visualization is a very powerful form of meditation. It's also comparatively easy since all the work is done for you: you just have to listen and visualize the images being described.

By the way, I'm using the terms guided meditation, guided visualization, guided imagery and mental rehearsal pretty interchangeably here.

Brain scans show that when we imagine an event, our thoughts "light up" the areas of the brain that are triggered during the actual event. So, the brain doesn't know the difference between an actual event and a visualization. This is why all professional athletes do mental practice, visualizing themselves performing their sport successfully, in addition to physical practicing.

A study in 2004 found that volunteers were able to increase muscle strength simply by imagining using the muscles. Some coaches even go as far as saying that sports are 90% mental and only 10% physical.

World champion golfer Jack Nicklaus is quoted as saying, "I never hit a shot, not even in practice, without having a very sharp in-focus picture of it in my head."

I once placed first in an equestrian event by having visualized myself riding the course at least 30 times before I ever got on the horse. When I did get on the horse, and in the arena, my brain and my body knew exactly what to do because it was as if they'd already ridden it 30 times! As a result, I came in first place! It was a personal best, because I was far from the best rider in my weekly classes. (I detail the story in the next chapter.)

So, if you see yourself relaxing in a beautiful garden, or at the beach, your body will respond as if it is there!

Research has established that guided imagery has a positive impact on health, creativity and performance. As little as 10 minutes of imagery can:

- Reduce blood pressure.
- Lower cholesterol and glucose levels in the blood.
- Heighten short-term immune cell activity.
- Reduce blood loss during surgery and morphine use after it.
- Lessen headaches and pain.
- Increase skills in skiing, skating, tennis, writing, acting and singing.
- Accelerate weight loss and reduce anxiety.

It has also been shown, again and again, to reduce the adverse effects of chemotherapy and radiation therapy, especially nausea, depression, soreness and fatigue.

UNDERSTANDING HOW WE RECEIVE INFORMATION

One of the things that may hold people back from trying guided meditations, or trying their own visualizations, is that they might feel they don't have strong visualization skills.

However, everyone can visualize, whether they think they can or not. If I ask you to describe your living room to me, you'll go into the visualization chambers of your brain to come up with the description.

So, there, you can visualize.

Even if you feel you have trouble visualizing, the other aspects of a guided meditation, such as the tone of the person's voice, or the background music, can lead you to deeply relax.

But I want to talk about how we receive intuitive information, so you don't judge yourself for not being able to visualize as well as the next person

We receive information in four primary ways:

- Visual (seeing)

- Auditory (hearing)

- Kinesthetic (feeling)

- Olfactory (Smell)

And we have preferences. Some people, in considering purchasing a new car, will want to test drive and feel the car move; others will be drawn by the look of the car; others by the sound of the engine and how quiet (or not) it is inside. Others will be most struck by the smell of the car's interior.

In learning or assessing anything, we will draw on those preferences.

I'm primarily visual and kinesthetic, so it's hard for me to buy clothes over the internet. I have to be able to touch and feel the fabric, and try the clothes on to feel how they fit.

President Lyndon Johnson was primarily auditory and that's how he liked to receive information. As a result, he had his staff read him reports because his brain would take the information in and retain it more readily by hearing it, rather than by reading.

Take a moment to consider how you like to receive information. Guided meditations will call on you to use your visual side, as well as the auditory.

If you're not primarily visual, perhaps you may find the music accompanying the meditation to be what relaxes you, or the sound of the person's voice.

If you're sensitive to smell, burning incense or spraying essential oils may be what works for you, or not.

Or without even visualizing the descriptions in the guided meditation, you may be able to tap into the relaxing feeling created.

I'm just suggesting you not rule out guided meditation simply because you don't think you can "visualize." My meditation, "You Are Light", which is referenced in the next lesson, contains visuals in addition to the soundtrack, for those people who would like to look at something to relax them, while they listen to the narration.

Exercise

Don't worry if you don't have enough time to listen to an entire meditation. Listen for as long as you can and you will still receive benefit.

My free guided meditation, "You Are Light", can be found on YouTube here: https://bit.ly/32sY6NZ.

It's just 7 minutes long. Give it a try. I also have a meditation CD that includes "You Are Light" along with two other meditations on it, available on my website here: https://mollylarkin.bandcamp.com/album/ancient-journeys

In my "Meditations on the Natural World" course, you will find another guided visualization: "Journey to a Sacred Garden."

After you've given one a try, write down your thoughts on guided visualization. How did the experience compare to the other approaches you've tried so far? Were you surprised that you could follow along, or did you have difficulties?

CHAPTER 19

Meditation/Visualization for Athletic Performance

"Believe you can and you will."

— MOLLY LARKIN

Some years ago, as an adult, I took up horseback riding. It was something I'd wanted to do for many years.

I was taking lessons at a stable in California that taught all levels, from children up to adults. Twice a year they held equestrian shows in which students were highly encouraged to participate.

I placed seventh in the first show I participated in, and I wasn't too happy about it. By the next show six months later, I wanted to do much better. I was jumping by this time so it would be a much more challenging event for me.

To guarantee a good outcome, the day before the show, I went to the stable office and got a copy of the layout of the course I was going to be riding. I went home and visualized riding it, over and over. I visualized how I'd enter the arena on the horse, how we'd approach each jump, where I'd change his lead, and how we'd stop at the end.

I probably rode that course at least 30 times in my head. So, the next day, it was practically effortless on my part to know exactly what to do and how to do it.

When I was at the gate ready to enter the arena, the coach said, "Start your trot when the rider in front of you reaches the last jump."

I was actually planning to canter the course and could have been thrown by her telling me to trot, but my mental vision was so clear on what I was to do, I didn't let her comment throw me.

I started my canter and went on to ride the course perfectly, winning the blue ribbon for that event and silver cup for overall best in my age group.

I don't tell you this story to boast, but to offer an example of what mental rehearsal can do. I was far from the best rider in any of my classes, but because of my preparation, I had a personal best.

As I've said before, visualization has long been a part of professional sports. Tennis star Billie Jean King beat Bobby Riggs in the famous "battle of the sexes" in the Houston Astrodome in 1973. She was using visualization in the 1960s, and athletes today are doing it more and more, with good reason:

According to the N.Y. Times:

"The practice of mentally simulating competition has become increasingly sophisticated, essential and elaborate, spilling over into realms like imagining the content of news conferences or the view from the bus window on the way to the downhill.

"Veteran American aerialist Emily Cook says it's more than visualization because you have to take in all the senses. 'You have to smell it. You have to hear it. You have to feel it, everything.'

"Imagery has seldom been more in evidence than at the 2014 Olympics in Sochi, where the starting areas were full of Olympians going through the motions, figuratively or literally. 'Oh, yeah, it's ridiculous; we're all up there flapping our arms,' Cook said. 'It looks insane, but it works.'" [**]

Injured athletes will also use imagery to see and feel their bones heal. It works because, again, the brain doesn't know the difference between imagery and a physical action. The same neurotransmitters fire in the brain whether you're visualizing or physically doing something.

Why am I including mental rehearsal for performance in a meditation book?

Because visualization is a form of meditation. And you need to cultivate the ability to control your mind if you're going to do this type of mental imagery for success, not only in sports, but in any endeavor.

You will need mental discipline in order to effectively practice mental imagery for successful performance and improved health. Rather than letting your wandering mind control your life, you can learn to control your mind.

[**]   Clarey, Christopher, "Olympians Use Imagery as Mental Training," N.Y. Times, February 22, 2014. https://www.nytimes.com/2014/02/23/sports/olympics/olympians-use-imagery-as-mental-training.html?_r=0

Meditation is the way to do it!

Exercise

1. What is something you do that you'd like to do better? Visualize yourself doing it successfully before you actually do it. Visualize consistently for five minutes a day and notice the results.

2. If you've tried it, how did it work out for you? Do you have a story to share that's similar to my equestrian show success?

3. You could also use this space to get started with your visualization by writing it down first.

CHAPTER 20
Coloring and Mandalas

"The mandala is a map for spiritual transformation."

— JUNE-ELLENI LAINE

It turns out coloring is not just for kids any more.

In December 2016, six of the twenty bestsellers on Amazon.com were coloring books!

Coloring mandalas has long been a favorite tool for relaxation and meditation.

A mandala is a spiritual and ritual symbol, often associated with Hinduism or Buddhism, that represents the universe. Mandalas are similar to the Celtic knots found all over Ireland, the place of my ancestors. Another description could be sacred geometric patterns.

Famed psychologist Carl Jung encouraged his patients to create mandalas at the turn of the last century, as a way of getting people to focus, relax and access the subconscious.

He also believed that coloring helped relieve patients' anxiety. We now know it has a lot of other stress-relieving qualities as well.

Mandalas aren't just for coloring. The ancients would gaze at mandalas as an aid to meditation used for focusing attention, and establishing sacred space.

Coloring for 30 minutes constitutes a focused meditation that relieves stress.

Psychologist Antoni Martínez recommends it as a relaxation technique: "We can use it to enter into a more creative, freer state. I recommend it in a quiet environment, even with chill music. Let the color and the lines flow."

Geometric patterns occur in nature all around us: the sun and moon, flowers, and snowflakes. According to the ancient science of Sacred Geometry, it is the pattern created by interlocking spheres that forms the matrix of all universal matter.

That sounds rather heady but, more simply put, geometric patterns represent harmony, unity, wholeness and healing—the interconnectedness of all life. The Lakota Sioux prayer, "Mitakuye oyasin", is a reflection of that teaching—that everything in nature is related.

The Irish are renowned for their Celtic knots—intricate, interwoven patterns that represent the same thing: the interconnectedness of all life. They are found in artwork and architecture all over Ireland.

To the Tibetans, the sand mandala represents multi-dimensional fields of spiritual consciousness and the state of enlightenment.

To Native Americans, the medicine wheel, a form of geometric pattern, symbolizes sacred ceremonial space and the circle of life.

Coloring brings the same benefits as any meditation practice, plus more:

- Balances your body, mind and spirit.
- Relieves tension and anxiety.
- Makes a spiritual connection.
- Expands creativity because it uses both sides of the brain.
- Increases your self-awareness.
- Encourages your self-expression.
- Improves organizational and fine motor skills.

Some of the other benefits are:

- No self-judgment because there's no right or wrong way to do it.
- There are no rules.
- You can color at your own pace.
- It's affordable.

ECOLOGICAL MANDALA COLORING TIPS

1. Sprout pencils, made with sustainable wood and fruit-and-vegetable based dyed clay instead of lead, are topped by non-GMO seeds that can be planted when the pencil becomes short.

2. Inktense's water-soluble brightly colored pencils mimic pen and ink; you can add water for translucency.

3. Select recycled paper books, soy crayons, watercolor paints and non-toxic markers.

4. You can download free coloring mandalas at: www.Printmandala.com

Exercise

Do it! (See the next page.)

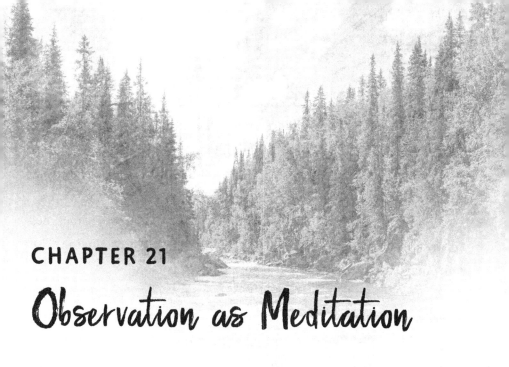

CHAPTER 21

Observation as Meditation

"Nature does not hurry, yet everything is accomplished."

— LAO TZU

Meditation doesn't have to be sitting inside with your eyes closed. Sitting outside with eyes and ears open and observing the world around us is a very powerful meditation.

It's also an important life skill. Being able to observe the world around us can be life-saving.

You can sit in one place and watch a bug, or a bird, or a squirrel. Watch birds in flight, flowers in their array of colors, or kittens playing. Listen to the wind. Any of these things can bring a wealth of joy and insight, and peace and calm.

But there's more to be gained than inner peace.

This can also be a way to rediscover your curiosity and wonderment in the world. We had it as children but as we age, it becomes less active.

How often do we slow down enough to practice simple observation? It will definitely achieve the same goal as more formal meditation: stilling the mind and opening up creativity and inspiration.

When the weather allows me to have the windows open, sometimes during my morning meditation, I just listen to the birds singing. Use your imagination to wonder what they're talking about!

In *The Wind Is My Mother: The Life and Teachings of a Native American Shaman*, Bear Heart shares how his tribe taught young people observation skills. Elders would take them out into the woods blindfolded and have them sit by a tree. They were told to stay there until the elder returned for them, and use the time to be with the tree, touching it, hugging it, leaning against it, getting to know it.

After half a day, the young person was brought back to camp, the blindfold removed, and told to go back out and find their tree! After touching a lot of trees, they could often find the one they sat beside. Those with highly developed intuition could go right to their tree, seeming to be drawn to it.

LISTENING TO THE WIND

A few years ago, I did something I've never done before. I ate my lunch without simultaneously reading or working; instead I ate on my screened porch and listened to the wind. Then I sat and listened some more.

It was a very strong wind; there were no other sounds to be heard over it. The birds that are usually so vocal during the day were relatively silent, perhaps holding onto tree branches for dear life. Native elders teach that the wind can bring us messages if we're paying attention.

One of the main forms of meditation practiced by indigenous people around the world is the observation of nature: watching, listening, feeling. It opens new experiences of communication with the natural world.

I think that most of us don't do enough of that, but it can open a lot of doors for us.

Exercises

1. Pick something pleasing to look at, something not moving, such as a candle flame, flower, plant or crystal. Focus on it with your eyes open for a few minutes. Then close your eyes and visualize it. You might find yourself merging into it, and it will bring you the same feeling of calm as comes with mindfulness practice.

2. Go out in nature and sit very still for as long as you can. Move your eyes very slowly from side to side. If you move too fast, you might startle some animals to flee. Watch a bug or bird or animal. What do you notice? Can you tell what direction the wind is coming from? What do you hear? What birds are you seeing? When you're motionless, birds and animals will feel safe to come closer. It can be both relaxing and educational. And deeply spiritual.

3. Write about your experience.

CHAPTER 22

Walking Meditation

"Meditation is a way for nourishing and blossoming the divinity within you."

— AMIT RAY

Walking… we do it every day, but how often do we do it mindfully? It's usually just a way to get where we're going, or it's considered exercise when we walk briskly.

But it's possible to meditate while walking, which might be a good technique for those who find it difficult to sit still for any period of time. Ideally, this will be done when you can walk without a destination or deadline.

Walking meditation has been practiced in monasteries around the world. If you can find a park to walk in, all the better, because you can also benefit from the beauty of nature. But, anywhere will work.

If the weather outside isn't appealing, walk inside your home.

Walking can become a meditation as long as you're not thinking your usual thoughts. So, don't walk and think. Walk and focus on your breath. Or say a mantra to keep your mind from wandering.

Here are some pointers:

- You're not going to necessarily change how you walk, you're just going to be aware of it. Perhaps walk slower than you would if you were exercising or on a mission to get somewhere.

- A basic walking meditation is to coordinate with your breath: take 4 steps for each inhale, and 4 steps with each exhale. Try to make your inhales and exhales the same length, if possible.

- Observe the act of your foot rising and coming down on the ground, of your legs moving forward. Reflect on the miracle of the human body. Notice how your heel strikes the ground first, then your foot rolls forward and the heel lifts.

- Each time your foot hits the ground, pay attention to your breath and the sensations in your body.

- Walk at a slow to moderate pace, arms at your sides. Gaze ahead.

- If your attention wanders, or you find yourself hurrying, just bring yourself back to focusing on walking and breathing.

- Walk this way for as long as you wish. 10–30 minutes is perfect.

One of the differences between sitting meditation and walking meditation is that in a sitting meditation, we are trying to shut out the outside world. In a walking meditation, we are embracing it.

Use a non-judgmental gaze to observe what's around you, taking in the sights as a non-judgmental observer. Be curious and be amazed by the world around you.

FOREST THERAPY

If you have the opportunity to walk in a forest, you will reap additional benefits.

Once again, scientists are proving what indigenous people and nature lovers have always known: being outdoors is healthy! Specifically, new research proves that being surrounded by a forest environment, what is called "forest therapy," can improve your health. It may even help fight cancer.

In Japan, forest therapy, or *shinrin-yoku*, is standard preventative medicine. It's not about being alone in the wilderness or extreme outdoor sports—it's about allowing your body and psyche to hang out in the peace of the woods.

The term *shinrin-yoku* was coined by the Japanese government in 1982, but is based on ancient Shinto and Buddhist practices. It's also known as "forest bathing."

It was just a few decades ago when people made fun of "tree huggers." As a former "tree hugger" myself, I now feel thoroughly vindicated!

THE RESEARCH ON "FOREST THERAPY"

Japanese researchers studying "forest therapy" have found measurable health benefits:

- Lower cortisol.
- Lower blood pressure.
- Reduced stress.
- Lower blood sugar.
- Improved concentration.
- Diminished pain.
- Improved immunity.
- Less depression and hostility.
- Increased vitality.
- Better concentration.
- Increased creativity.

Japan has 48 official Forest Therapy Trails with scientifically documented relaxing effects. It intends to designate a total of 100 Forest Therapy Sites within the next 10 years.

Results are so pronounced that some Japanese companies are starting to include forest therapy in employee health care benefits. Also, wellness programs with free check-ups are available inside Japanese forests.

IN MORE RESEARCH...

Three days of hiking and camping in the wilderness increased creativity scores by 50%, according to a joint study by the University of Kansas and University of Utah.

U.S. research on children with attention-deficit/hyperactivity disorder (ADHD) found that children experienced substantially improved concentration after a 20-minute walk in a city park as compared to a

20-minute walk in downtown or residential settings. The researchers concluded the positive results were comparable to the effects of Ritalin— yet more incentive for parents to get children outdoors and away from electronic screens.

Even just gazing at forest scenery for 20 minutes reduces salivary cortisol levels by 13.4%. Cortisol is the "stress hormone" that over prolonged periods can suppress the immune system, along with other negative effects.

FOREST THERAPY INCREASES OUR NATURAL KILLER CELLS

Natural killer immune cells (NK cells) are a type of white blood cell which sends self-destruct messages to tumors and virus-infected cells, including cancer cells. It's known that stress, aging and pesticides can reduce our NK count.

Forest therapy has been found to increase NK cells, which can be reliably measured in a lab and are, therefore, an excellent research subject.

Researchers found that spending three days in the forest increases NK activity by 40% and that the benefit can last up to one month.

WHY FOREST THERAPY WORKS

A recent study from UK researchers at Heriot-Watt University in Scotland found that the brain enters a meditative state when one is in "green space."

The Japanese father of forest therapy is Miyazaki, a physiological anthropologist and vice director of Chiba University's Center for

Environment, Health and Field Sciences. He believes that because humans evolved in nature, it's where we are most comfortable, even if we don't always know it:

> "Our physiological functions are still adapted to it. During everyday life, a feeling of comfort can be achieved if our rhythms are synchronized with those of the environment."

Exercise:

1. Go for a "Nature Walk" to enhance your intuition via walking meditation:

> The universe is constantly talking to us if we listen. Before going for a walk in nature, put out a question, something for which the answer has eluded you. Say,
>
> WHAT DO I NEED TO KNOW ABOUT _____
>
> Then go for a walk, being observant of the world around you. Somewhere on that walk, you will see, feel or hear something that will give you your answer: a bird in flight, a critter scurrying under a shrub, bugs on the march....
> Allow nature to speak to you, because it will.
> I've done this many times with my students: it always works! And it's an excellent exercise for opening your intuition.

2. Try a walking meditation while focusing on the breath: Walk slowly, matching your inhales and exhales with the walk: four steps for each inhale; four steps for each exhale. If that count doesn't work for you, find one that does. The important thing is to keep your mind from wandering and find something to focus on. Breathing is an excellent focal point.

3. What did Nature tell you? Write about what you saw, heard, felt, or smelled.

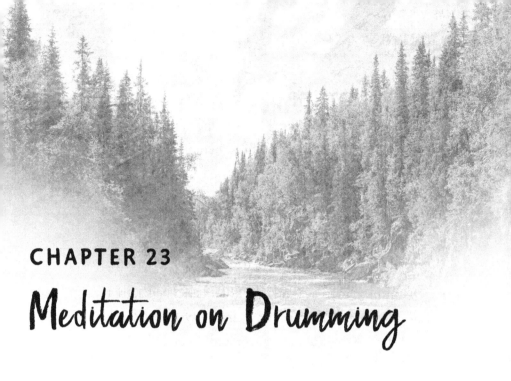

CHAPTER 23
Meditation on Drumming

"The drum is the heartbeat of Mother Earth. Be one with her."

— BEAR HEART

I facilitated Full Moon Drumming Circles for many years and I always got the same comment when new people inquired about joining us: "I've never drummed before and don't know how to do it."

The fact is, everyone knows how to drum. Our ancestors did it. It's in our genes and is one of the oldest means of meditation, communication, healing, and musical expression.

I just tell newcomers to relax, keep a steady beat and follow the leader. Nothing could be simpler.

HEALTH BENEFITS OF DRUMMING

The health benefits of drumming are similar to those of meditation, and also include some documented medical benefits:

- Reduces the hormonal stress response.
- Helps reduce depression and boosts health.
- Participants in weekly drumming sessions were less anxious, less distressed and had higher self-esteem.
- Drumming increases natural killer (NK) cell activity and therefore enhances the immune system. (Remember that the NK cells attack cancer and other cells that don't belong in your body.)
- Alzheimer's patients who drum can connect better with loved ones. Research shows that the brain forms new neurological pathways when performing arts and music.
- Rhythmic cues can help retrain the brain after stroke.
- Improves concentration.
- Reduces inflammation in the body.
- Some hospitals take percussion instruments into patients' rooms and invite them to play as a way of relieving pain and stress, and helping them engage socially.

Keep in mind that drums are sacred instruments often used in prayer and healing ceremonies throughout the world. The elders teach that, in most drums, the frame came from a tree that was formerly living, while the skin came from an animal that was once alive and gave of itself for us to use. So, we should respect it that way.

In our drumming circles, there is usually silence in between drumming rounds, because the peaceful energy created by the drumming, along with the unity of the circle, is a beautiful meditation.

Both the sound of the drum and the sound of stillness is the sound of the Divine.

Exercises

1. If you have a drum of any kind, just sit down and drum. You'll find yourself entering a sacred, meditative space.

2. In my meditation course, I play a Maya drum beat you can drum along with. You can either listen or, if you have a drum, join in and drum along.

3. Write and reflect about your experience of drumming. Is this a practice you will continue? Have you considered joining a drumming circle nearby?

CHAPTER 24

Meditation on Sacred Fire

"Ceremonial fire is a gift from the Creator. It is spirit made manifest. Send your prayers up with the smoke."

— **MOLLY LARKIN**

Fire is magical, otherworldly, and a beautiful thing upon which to focus our attention.

Yes, it can get out of hand and be destructive but, more often than not, it is peaceful and contained.

What is more relaxing than sitting and watching a fire?

We've all had the experience of being mesmerized by a fire. There's a reason you can buy a DVD of a flickering fire to play on your TV!

It transfixes and transports us. So it is a perfect vehicle for meditation.

Many years ago I was babysitting my one-year-old nephew who was getting cranky and nothing was working to calm him down.

Then I lit the candles on my angel chimes. The heat of the candle flame causes the angels above to fly around in a circle and he was transfixed by the angels and the candle flame and calmed right down.

Sacred Fire can calm us all down.

I don't believe I have ever been to a Native American ceremony that did not incorporate Sacred Fire.

Here are some Native American teachings about fire:

- Fire is a gift from the Creator. It is spirit made manifest.

- It is untouchable yet touches us with its warmth and light.

- When we learn how to communicate with it, our lives are enriched.

- Ancient cultures used the fire for divination, and to communicate with other realms.

- Bear Heart and other Native Americans I know would read the coals for information and messages. And they would send their prayers out on the smoke, to be carried up to the Creator.

- The ancient Celts would keep the hearth fire lit year round. It was only allowed to die on the Beltane festival on the First of May, when it was ritually rekindled.

The hearth fire was the center of Native American and Celtic family life. Just as the sun provides warmth and light, and allows growing things to flourish, fire warms our homes and cooks our food, and lights our way in the dark.

Evening storytelling would take place around the warmth of the fire, as its light played with shadows and created a mystical environment.

If you have an indoor or outdoor fireplace, this can be a perfect place to meditate. By mindfully building and tending the fire, and gazing upon its beauty, you can quiet the mind.

Even a candle will do. Just gaze at it, trying to empty your mind of thoughts. Notice the color of the flame and the candle, how it flickers. Imagine the light spreading, enveloping you in light, and then moving on to envelop the whole world in light.

Exercise

1. Light a candle in a dimly lit room, sit comfortably, and just observe it as a meditation, while focusing on your breath. It moves and flows, yet stays constantly there, which is a perfect analogy for the meditating mind.

2. Write your reflections on what you feel, see, and hear during this practice.

Epilogue

I trust you have found a practice in here that resonates with you, and brings you peace of mind.

I also hope I've gotten across the point that there's not just "one way to meditate."

Even after you find one that works for you, try others to broaden your perspective.

Wishing you wonderful meditations!

Best,
Molly

Bibliography

Bear Heart and Molly Larkin, *The Wind Is My Mother; The Life and Teachings of a Native American Shaman.* Random House, 1996.

Brooks, Katherine, "Coloring Isn't Just for Kids. It Can Actually Help Adults Combat Stress." Huffpost.com, 10/13/14. https://www.huffing tonpost.com/2014/10/13/coloring-for-stress_n_5975832.html

CBS News, "How meditation is making a 'huge difference' in one Baltimore School." https://www.cbsnews.com/news/meditation-stu dents-mindful-moments-program-robert-w-coleman-elementary-school/ October 26, 2016.

Chen, Wen G., Ph.D., "Mindfulness Meditation Reduces Pain, Bypasses Opioid Receptors." NCCIH Research Blog, March 16, 2016. https://nccih.nih.gov/research/blog/mindfulness-meditation-pain

Cimperman, Sarah, N.D., "Forest Therapy." A Different Kind of Doctor blog, October 4, 2010, http://adifferentkindofdoctor.blogspot.com/2010/10/forest-therapy.html

Clarey, Christopher, "Olympians Use Imagery as Mental Training," N.Y. Times, February 22, 2014. https://www.nytimes.com/2014/02/23/sports/olympics/olympians-use-imagery-as-mental-training.html?_r=0

Clear, James, "The Ivy Lee Method: The Daily Routine Experts Recommend for Peak Productivity." https://jamesclear.com/ivy-lee

Erin Elizabeth, "Group drumming more effective than antidepressants, study suggests." August 31, 2016, https://www.healthnutnews.com/group-drumming-effective-antidepressants-study-suggests/

Frank, Priscilla, "Why Coloring Could Be The New Alternative to Meditation." Huffpost.com, July 30, 2015. http://www.huffingtonpost.com/entry/coloring-benefits-meditation_us_55b7c9c1e4b0074ba5a6724f

Gallwey, W. Timothy, *The Inner Game of Tennis: The Classic Guide to the Mental Side of Peak Performance*. Random House, 1974.

Gaynor, Mitchell L., M.D., *The Healing Power of Sound; Recovery from Life-threatening Illness Using Sound, Voice and Music.* Shambhala Publications, 1999, p. 13.

Giovanni, "Scientific Benefits of Meditation—76 things you might be missing out on." http://liveanddare.com/benefits-of-meditation/

Healthline, "Does Music Affect Your Mood?" https://www.healthline.com /health-news/mental-listening-to-music-lifts-or-reinforces-mood-051713#3

Herbert, Anne and Esparham, Anna, "Mind-Body Therapy for Children with ADHD." Children (Basel) 2017 May; 4(5): 31. Published online 2017 Apr 25. doi: 10.3390/children4050031 PMCID: PMC5447989

https://www.ncbi.nlm.nih.gov/pmc/articles/PMC5447989/

Higher Perspectives, "Psychologists Say Coloring Is the Best Alternative to Meditation." Oct. 15, 2015, https://www.nytimes.com/2014/02/23 /sports/olympics/olympians-use-imagery-as-mental-training.html?_r=0

Howard, Jacqueline, "Americans devote more than 10 hours a day to screen time, and growing." CNN.com, July 29, 2016, https://www.cnn .com/2016/06/30/health/americans-screen-time-nielsen/index.html

Infante, Jose R, et al., "Levels of immune cells in transcendental medita-tion practitioners." International Journal of Yoga, July–Dec. 2014. 7(2): 147–151. doi: 10.4103/0973-6131.133899 PMCID: PMC4097901

John, Tara, "Doctors are prescribing nature to patients in the UK's Shetland Islands." CNN.com, October 5, 2018. https://www.cnn .com/2018/10/05/health/nature-prescriptions-shetland-intl/index.html

Kenney, Tanasia, "This Baltimore Elementary School Swaps Detention for Mindful Meditation—the Results Are Amazing." Atlanta Black Star, September 29, 2016. http://atlantablackstar.com/2016/09/29 /this-baltimore-elementary-school-swaps-detention-for-mindful-med itation-the-results-are-amazing/

Killingsworth, Matthew A. and Gilbert, Daniel T., "A Wandering Mind Is An Unhappy Mind." *Science Magazine*, 12 Nov. 2010, vol. 330, Issue 6006, pp. 932.

Larkin, Molly, *The Fountain of Youth is Just A Breath Away: Breathing Exercises for Relaxation, Health and Vitality*. Four Winds Press, 2015.

Mack, Avery, "Color Me Calm," *Natural Awakenings*, West Michigan Edition, March 2016.

McTaggart, Lynne, *The Field, The Quest for the Secret Force of the Universe*. Harper, 2008.

Newberg, Andrew, D'Aquili, Eugene, and Rause, Vince, *Why God Won't Go Away; Brain Science and the Biology of Belief*. Ballantine Books, 2002.

NIH National Cancer Institute, Dictionary of Cancer Terms, "Natural Killer Cell." https://www.cancer.gov/publications/dictionaries/cancer-terms/def/natural-killer-cell

Print Mandala, www.printmandala.com

Project Resiliency, Mind-Body-Drum. "The Benefits of Drumming." https://project-resiliency.org/resiliency/the-benefits-of-druming/

Rankin, Lissa, M.D., *Mind Over Medicine; Scientific Proof That You Can Heal Yourself.* Hay House, 2013.

Sboros, Marika, "Placebo magic in medicine—why deep relaxation is key." https://www.biznews.com/health/2014/03/14/placebo-magic-medicine-deep-relaxation-response-answer

Schulte, Brigid, "Harvard neuroscientist: Meditation not only reduces stress, here's how it changes the brain." Washington Post, May 26, 2015. https://www.washingtonpost.com/news/inspired-life/wp/2015/05/26/harvard-neuroscientist-meditation-not-only-reduces-stress-it-literally-changes-your-brain/

Siegler, MG, "Eric Schmidt: Every 2 Days We Create As Much Information As We Did Up to 2003." https://techcrunch.com/2010/08/04/schmidt-data/

The Japanese Tea Ceremony, http://japanese-tea-ceremony.net

Vrancken, Steven, "Your introduction to the Healing Powers of Mandala Coloring Pages." https://mandalacoloringmeditation.com /mandala-coloring/mandala-articles/about-mandala-coloring-healing/

Wake Forest Baptist Medical Center, "'Mindful People Feel Less Pain; MRI Imaging Pinpoints Supporting Brain Activity." September 5, 2018, https://newsroom.wakehealth.edu /News-Releases/2018/09/Mindful-People-Feel-Less-Pain

Walton, Alice G. "Science Shows Meditation Benefits Children's Brains and Behavior." Forbes Magazine, October 18, 2016. https://www.forbes.com/sites/alicegwalton/2016/10/18 /the-many-benefits-of-meditation-for-children/#e724bebdbe33

WebMD, "The Effects of Stress on Your Body." https://www.webmd.com /balance/stress-management/effects-of-stress-on-your-body

Wheeler, Mark, "Forever young: Meditation might slow the age-related loss of gray matter in the brain." UCLA Newsroom, February 5, 2015, http:// newsroom.ucla.edu/releases/forever-young-meditation-might-slow -the-age-related-loss-of-gray-matter-in-the-brain-say-ucla-researchers

Williams, Florence, "Take Two Hours of Pine Forest and Call Me in the Morning," Outside Magazine, November 28, 2012. https://www.outsideonline.com/1870381 /take-two-hours-pine-forest-and-call-me-morning?page=2

World Peace Group. "Washington crime study shows 23.3% drop in violent crime trend due to meditating group." http://www.worldpeace group.org/washington_crime_study.html

Yoga4classrooms.com, Supporting Research. http://www.yoga4class rooms.com/supporting-research

About the Author

Molly Larkin has been a spiritual seeker and student of human potential since the age of seven, when her teacher said human beings only use 10% of their brain capacity. She decided then and there to learn to use 100% of hers, a decision which led her on a life-long spiritual quest.

She has been an avid practitioner of meditation for many years. This book is the companion piece to her online meditation course, "Meditations on the Natural World."

Her previous books are the international best-seller, *The Wind Is My Mother: The Life and Teachings of a Native American Shaman,* co-authored with Muskogee Creek elder Marcellus "Bear Heart" Williams, and *The Fountain of Youth is Just a Breath Away: Breathing Exercises for Relaxation, Health and Vitality.* She also created a guided meditation CD, *Ancient Journeys.* All are available on Amazon.

She has studied with indigenous elders from around the world for over 30 years. Her passion for health and healing led her to become a certified spiritual healing practitioner and licensed tutor for NFSH—The Healing Trust, England's oldest and largest spiritual healing organization.

In her private healing practice, Molly works with people, pets and horses, both in person and long distance, helping them achieve emotional, spiritual and physical balance.

Molly's mission is to help students and clients achieve their life purpose and lead a balanced life through living on this planet in harmony with the earth and one another. In other words, to help people live at 100% of their own potential.

You can receive ongoing teachings and inspiration by subscribing to her blog, "Ancient Wisdom for Balanced Living," at www.MollyLarkin .com.

Made in the USA
Coppell, TX
04 April 2020

18462545R00105